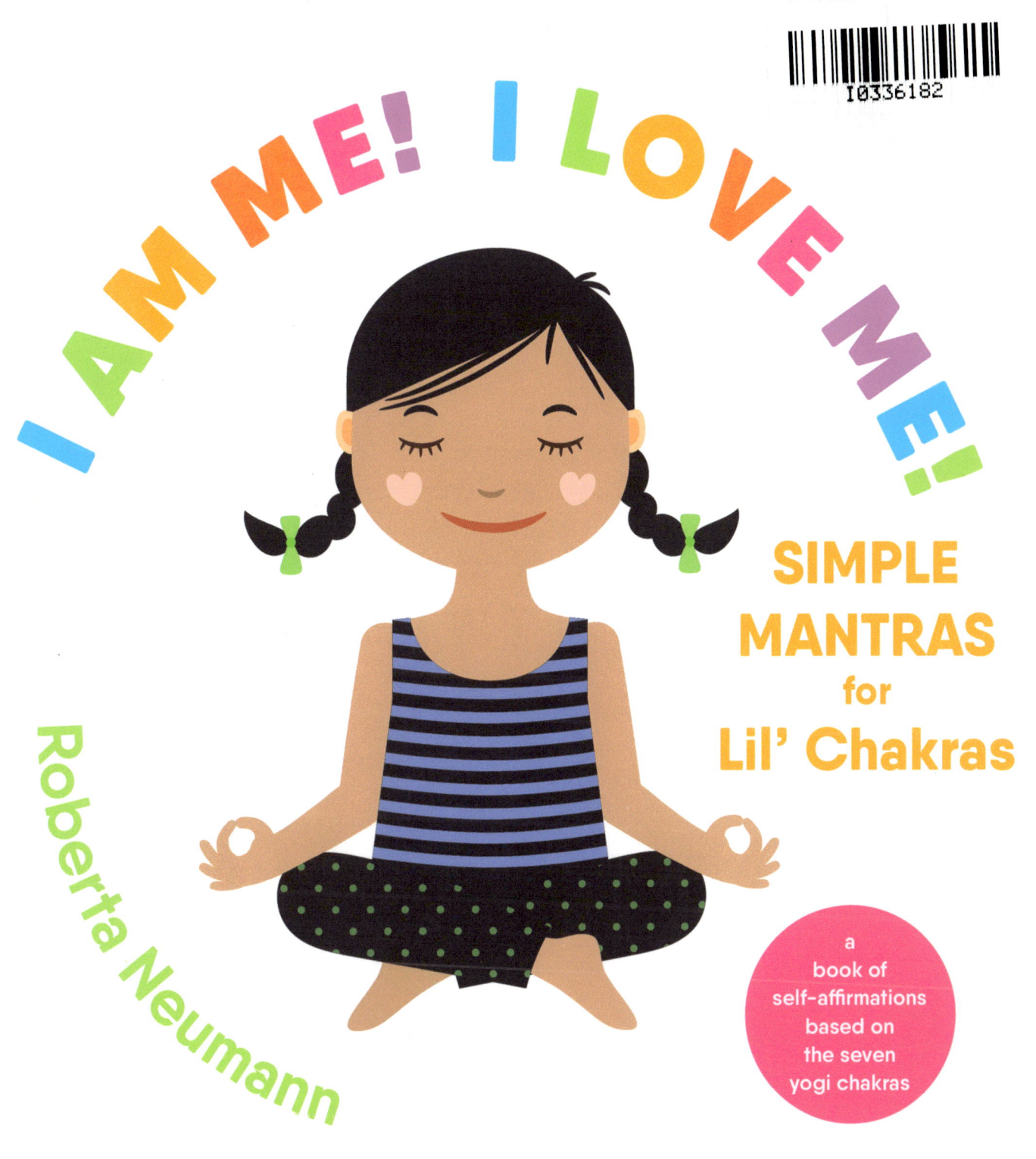

ABOUT THE AUTHOR
ROBERTA NEUMANN

Roberta Neumann is a master health and physical education teacher and a wellness and yoga instructor. She loves physical activity, the outdoors, travel, and reading. She and her family have lived in Asia, Europe, and the United States. She has three active adult children, a Wheaton Terrier named Gizmo, and a goofy husband.

Copyright 2021 © Roberta Neumann

Publisher: Roberta Neumann

Publishing and Design Services: MelindaMartin.me

All rights reserved. No part of this book may be used or reproduced in any manner whatsoever without prior written permission of the author/publisher, except in the case of brief quotations embodied in reviews.

Pronunciation guide: https://satyayogacooperative.com/sanskrit-pronunciation-guide-chakras

Dedication

This book is dedicated to all those who struggle with self-love. And, to my mom and dad who have always inspired me and instilled a love for children, learning and reading. To my three strong-willed children and supportive husband, thank you for loving me. And lastly, to all the little yogis out there, may you have fun and find peace in your journey. The light in me honors the light in you.

Namaste.

Root Chakra
MOUNTAIN POSE

I AM ME!
I am strong, beautiful, and able.
I am solid, sturdy, and mighty.
I am brave.
I am powerful.
I LOVE ME!

BREATHE AND BELIEVE.

Third Eye Chakra
EAGLE POSE

I AM ME!
I am clever, smart and aware.
I listen.
I hear.
I see.
I can hear, feel and see my breath.
I LOVE ME!

BREATHE AND BELIEVE.

Solar Plexus Chakra
ALLIGATOR POSE

I AM ME!
I meet and greet.
I am grateful, thankful,
and positive.
I am brave.
I LOVE ME!

BREATHE AND BELIEVE.

Heart Chakra
SNAKE POSE

I AM ME!
I see, hear, smell, and taste.
I am watchful and mindful.
I am good and caring.
I am accepting and kind.
I LOVE ME!

BREATHE AND BELIEVE.

Crown Chakra
PIGEON POSE

I AM ME!
I am physical, natural and earthy.
I am mindful of me.
I am peace and love.
I am a treasure.
I LOVE ME!

BREATHE AND BELIEVE.

Heart Chakra
CAMEL POSE

I AM ME!
Calm and free as can be.
A giver and receiver of love.
Open mind, thoughtfully kind.
Stress and strain can be a gain.
I LOVE ME!

BREATHE AND BELIEVE.

Third Eye Chakra
BUTTERFLY POSE

I AM ME!
I am diverse.
I see colors.
My colors are bright.
I am what I see.
I LOVE ME!

BREATHE AND BELIEVE.

Sacral Chakra
TURTLE POSE

I AM ME!
I have feelings.
Some are anxious, scared,
angry, sad, and hurt.
Others are excited, joyful,
peaceful, silly, and energetic.
I LOVE ME!

BREATHE AND BELIEVE.

Crown Chakra
RAINBOW POSE

I AM ME!
The world is big.
The earth is splendid.
The world is divine.
The earth is colorful just like me.
I LOVE ME!

BREATHE AND BELIEVE.

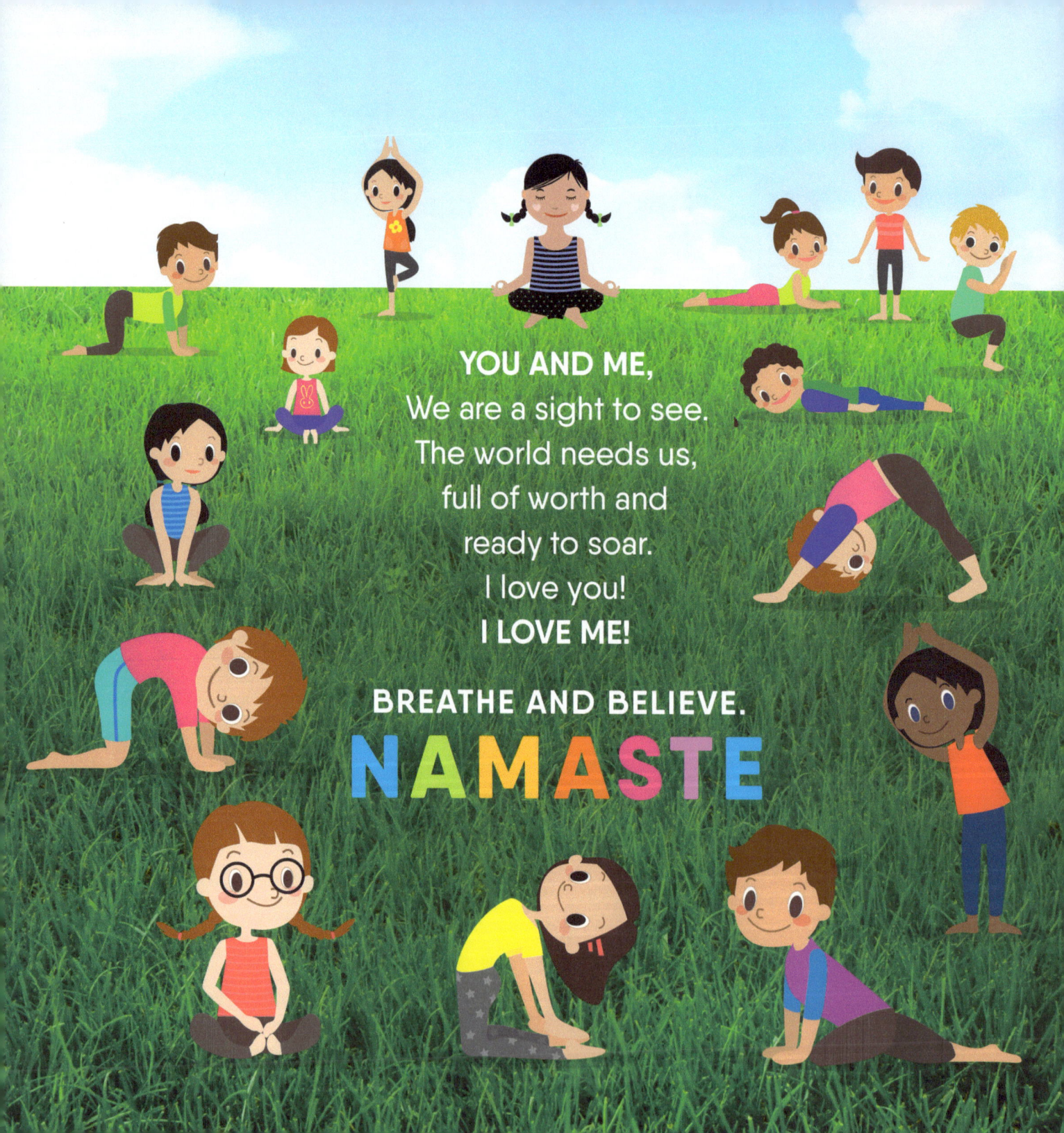

DEFINITIONS

Believe — Accepting something is true, with or without proof.

Breathe — To take a breath, take air into the lungs through the mouth or nose and blow it out.

Chakras — The chakras are energy centers in our bodies through which energy flows. There are seven chakras. These energy centers should stay open. They support body organs and nerves, which can affect emotional and physical well-being.

Exhale — To breathe out.

Inhale — To breathe in.

Mantra — An idea or fact that is mentioned repeatedly, especially in encouragement.

Namaste — Phrase used at the end of a yoga class meaning "the light in me honors the light in you". Acknowledging and honoring the beauty, love, truth and peace in ourselves and others.

Pranayama — A yogi practice focusing on the art of controlled breathing and increasing energy flow through the body.

Sanskirt — An ancient language of India.

Yoga — A discipline which focuses on using breathing techniques, bodily postures, exercise and meditation to improve health and happiness. It is both spiritual and physical.

Yogi — Someone who is committed to the practice of yoga.

GET READY TO EXPLORE FUN BREATHING EXERCISES

7 CHAKRAS & **14 YOGA POSES**

BREATHING EXERCISES

INHALE.....EXHALE.....

Respect each breath

"If you breathe well,
you will live long on the earth."
—Indian Proverb

 Healing benefits for breathing practices

Decreases stress.

Reduces anxiety.

Helps you remain calm.

Strengthens sustained attention.

Sharpens the ability to focus and learn.

Slows the heart rate.

Lowers blood pressure.

Helps control your emotions.

BREATHING ACTIVITIES FOR CHILDREN

Use your imagination and listen to your breath while practicing these breathing activities. Repeat these exercises as often as you like.

Balloon Breathing
Sit comfortably in a cross-legged position and cup your hands around your mouth. Inhale deeply through the nose and then purse your lips while slowly exhaling through your mouth and into your hands like you are blowing up a balloon.

Blowing Bubbles
Take a deep breath in and blow out soft and long like you're blowing a nice big bubble.

Bumble Bee Breath
Sit comfortably and inhale through your nose. Keeping your mouth closed, make a humming or buzzing noise (like a bumblebee) while you exhale. You can also cup your hands over your ears to amplify the buzzing sound.

 ### Bunny Breath

This activity can be done while sitting or moving.

Sitting: Make "bunny" hands in front of your chest and like a bunny take quick sniffs in through your nose 5-7 times, then one long exhale.

Moving: Stand in a squat position and hop forward while taking quick bunny sniffs through your nose 5-7 times, then one long exhale.

 ### Color Breathing

Breathe in and imagine a beautiful, bright, calm, happy, color. Breathe out and imagine a color which represents stress and anxiety leaving your body.

 ### Cowabunga Breathing

Block one nostril with your pointer finger. Breathe in for a 5 second count. Block other nostril with your pointer finger and breathe out for a 5 second count. Switch sides and repeat.

 ### Straw Breathing

Pretend you have a straw in your mouth. Suck in through the straw breathing in. Blow into the straw breathing out.

 ### Deep Belly Breath

Place one hand on your chest and one hand on your belly. Take a deep breath in for four counts and then exhale slowly (through your nose) for four counts. Notice and pay attention to the rise and fall of your belly and chest.

Deep Breathing With Numbers

Count to 10 while breathing in (inhale). Count to 10 again while breathing out (exhale). Repeat with 7, 5, and 4 counts.

Dragon Fire Breath

Interlace your fingers under your chin and raise your elbows as high as you can around your neck and face as you inhale. As you exhale, lower your elbows back down. Be fierce like a dragon!

Explosion Breath

Start in a standing position. Breathe in as you crouch down. Then jump up, spreading your arms and legs as you breathe out. Explode!

Hands To Shoulders

While taking a deep breath in, put your hands on your shoulders and notice whether your shoulders are moving a lot.

If your shoulders are moving, focus more on taking breaths using your belly and keeping your shoulders more still.

Lion Roar

Begin on your knees, then sit back on your heels. Press your hands onto your knees and spread your fingers wide. Take a deep breath in through your nose, open your mouth and eyes wide, and ROAR! Like a lion.

Volcano Breath

Begin with your hands in front of your heart with palms touching. Keeping your hands together, reach straight up while breathing in. Separate your hands and move your arms down to your side and breath out. Pretend your hands and arms are lava flowing from a volcano.

Ocean Breathing

Imagine you are a wave rolling into shore. Inhale, then exhale, making a crashing sound.

Rainbow Breathing

Start with your arms at the side of your body; arms go up as you breathe in and go down as you breathe out (arms make a rainbow).

Shoulder Roll Breath

Shoulder roll breaths are a great breathing exercise with the added benefit of releasing tight muscles and tension. Sit comfortably and take a deep breath in. Roll your shoulders up toward your ears. Then drop your shoulders back down as you exhale.

Smell the Flower and Blow Out the Candle

Pretend you have a flower in one hand and a candle in the other. First smell the flower by taking a deep breath in through the nose and fill your lungs with air. Next, exhale through your mouth, blowing out the candle in the other hand.

Snake Breath

Breathe in deeply, pause, then breathe out slowly while you make a hissing sound for as long as you can.

Whale Breath

Sitting in a cross-legged position, sit up tall, and take a deep breath in through your nose. Hold it while you count to 5, then tilt your head up to blow out your blowhole (your mouth). You can also put your hands on top of your head, making a circle with your hands to create the blow hole.

Wood Chopper Breathing

Stand tall with your legs hip-distance apart. Clasp hands together and raise your arms above your head. Breathe in through your nose. While you exhale pull your hands down toward your legs like you are chopping wood and say "HA."

ROOT CHAKRA

Muladhara
("moolah"-thAA-ruh)

CHAKRA 1
ROOT CHAKRA

Grounded • Secure • Safety • Basic Trust

SACRAL CHAKRA

Svadhisthana
(svAA-thiSH-TAA-nuh)

CHAKRA 2
SACRAL CHAKRA

Creativity • Self-Expression • Emotional Stability

SOLAR PLEXUS CHAKRA

Manipura
("money"-poo-ruh)

CHAKRA 3
SOLAR PLEXUS CHAKRA

Wisdom • Power • Purpose • Self-Esteem

HEART CHAKRA

Anahata
(un-AA-huh-THuh)

CHAKRA 4
HEART CHAKRA

Love • Healing • Kindness • Empathy

THROAT CHAKRA

Vishuddha
(vish-shoo-dda)

CHAKRA 5
THROAT CHAKRA

Speech • Hearing • Communication

THIRD EYE CHAKRA

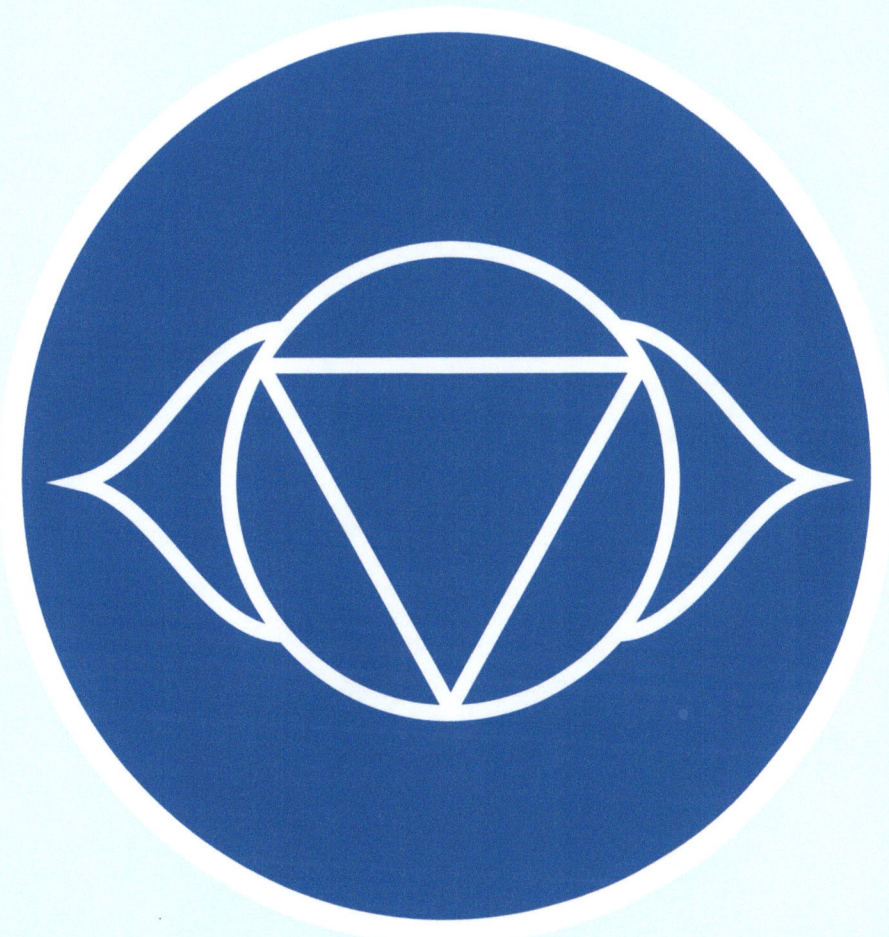

Ajña
(AAg-nyuh) or (AAg-yuh)

CHAKRA 6
THIRD EYE CHAKRA

Awareness • Mind and Body Together • Intuition

CROWN CHAKRA

Sahasrara
(suh-huss-rAA-ruh)

CHAKRA 7
CROWN CHAKRA

Enlightenment • Spirituality

HOW DO THE COLORS MAKE YOU FEEL?